Praise for
20 Self-Care Habits

20 Habits of Self-Care is exactly what it says on the cover—a book about self-care habits, and I absolutely loved it. Once I started reading it, I couldn't put it down, not just because it was so interesting but also because of how easy it was to read.

After introducing us to the subject of self-care and why it is so important, the author begins each chapter with a quote related to the topic being discussed, which immediately got me thinking about the subject and how it relates to my own life. The friendly, natural writing style enabled me to really reflect on how each self-care tip already does or could improve my life, and the personal experiences she shares throughout the book also helped with this.

Each chapter relates to a different self-care practice, all of which could be easily incorporated into even the busiest of people's lives because of their simplicity. What I really enjoyed is that the author doesn't just introduce us to the concepts of self-care practices but also makes suggestions about how, by using these practices every day, we can experience improvements in both our lives and our relationships. She allows us to think about the importance of putting our own needs in front of those of others and reminds us that saying no isn't a bad thing.

The reflective exercises at the end of each chapter provided me a fantastic opportunity to really sit and think about how when I haven't put my own needs first, it has negatively impacted my self-esteem or feelings of self-worth and how differently things could have been if I had. Including these exercises meant that I didn't just rush onto the next chapter, and by slowing the reading process down in this way, it felt like the author was already encouraging me to slow down the pace I normally live my life.

As mentioned previously, the author's personal reflections really helped me really reflect on the importance of self-care, but not only that, but they also made the whole idea of self-care more relatable to everyday life.

Whether you are new to the idea of self-care or an old hand, this book is a light, easy read.. Having already noticed the changes it has made to my life since reading it, I highly recommend it.

—Maz. C.

In the opening chapters, *20 Habits of Self-Care* makes a bold claim that by implementing some of the activities from the book into our lives, we can expect to lead an improved life. I was sceptical of this claim at first, but by the time I had reached the end of the book, I could see how by implementing some of the activities and ideas that most resonated with me, I could expect to see an increase in my mental well-being.

Often, when we think of self-care, we think of treating ourselves, whether that be to make something nice to eat or time doing an activity we enjoy. Whilst this can fulfil part of our individual self-care needs, the self-care habits in this book go deeper than this and are about shaping our overall well-being rather than a quick pick-me-up. The "habits" are ideas that can be implemented into one's life and therefore become the everyday, rather than a special treat.

One idea that resonated with me personally was the concept of personal space in relation to technology.

Technology and personal space are not something I have put together before, and this has encouraged me to have some downtime from my mobile phone. Perhaps I will have my time away from technology whilst spending time in nature, really focusing on my surroundings rather than hiking through a park with my headphones on, thinking that I have "done" nature for the day.

There is a running theme throughout of improving self-esteem, and I would say that this book is ideal for someone who is looking to boost their mental well-being and/ or self-esteem. If you are someone who is suffering from depression, implementing some of the activities in this book may well be very useful for you, but self-care may begin with fulfilling basic needs such as looking after health and hygiene. In that case, this book may be the next step.

This book appears to be written from Karin's own journey of self-care. A lot of examples are written from her own personal experience, which gives credibility and integrity to the ideas that are discussed. I particularly liked the practical nature of this book. It's concise but has many ideas for personal reflection (making it personal to each reader) and practical ideas on how to implement some of the habits into your life. Rather than being a theoretical book that is read and then stays on the shelf, I can see how the activities and ideas could become part of the everyday for both myself and my clients.

—Claire. B.

Karin Brauner's *20 Habits of Self-Care* is the only book you will need to buy on self-care. Whether this is the first time you have dipped your toe in the world of wellness and self-care or you are well-versed on the subject, this is the only book you'll ever need. Well written with easy-to-follow instructions on how to reframe your life, this is a self-care book with a difference.

The author is honest with the reader right from the beginning; she doesn't sugar coat the reality that living your true life will require hard work and dedication to understanding yourself. That is just one of the reasons why this book is different from the rest; she is not offering a quick fix. There are, of course, little exercises that can be done in times of needs, but she is offering much more than that. She is offering a mindset reset, one that will change your whole life, and you'll finish the book knowing yourself better than you ever thought possible.

The book starts by concentrating on the importance of boundaries in your life and highlights the tools needed to start structuring your own life with boundaries, dealing with your mind, body, spirit, and relationships. You will learn how to structure your life in a way that is dictated by your needs and not societal demands.

As you realise that you too are worthy of happiness, the author guides you through the difficult relationships you may have to navigate by not shying away from conflict. Instead, she meets them head-on, bringing about a new respect for both you and your relationships.

Each chapter has a different theme that you can dip into at any time you are struggling with that particular issue in your life. You are given tips for improving the situation, but more importantly, how to reduce the likelihood of coming across these situations again— you will have learned the tools to deal with the next step when needed. Each theme is fully explored, then you will be lead through a series of visualisation exercises and given options for alternative outcomes. It's the ultimate learning tool.

As you continue your journey into self-awareness, it will become easier to identify old patterns and make new behaviours. The author gives you the power to say no, and in a world where saying yes is the only answer, you are helped to take back your power and own your own destiny and regain that control of your life.

Through a series of visualisation exercises, meditations, reframing, and life hacks, you will learn how to take responsibility for your decisions. You will end up confident in your identity and living a life that is true to who you are at the core. You learn how to trust yourself. After all, who knows you better than you do? It's time to start listening to yourself, and this book gives you the tools to do so.

—A.L.

20 Self-Care Habits is a practical and insightful tool for anyone who wants to make self-care a priority.

The overall message is much the same as other self-care books; however, it is original in the reflection aspect. The think, feel, and act sections are good prompts for anyone new to reflection in this sense.

I would say the book is aimed at beginners in self-care, and it is a great place to start. It could be all that a "newbie" to self-care requires. As someone who has been reading other self-care books and undertaking reflections for over three years, a lot of the features were what I have already been introduced to. That being said, the think, feel, and act sections drew my attention to specific areas of reflection that I had not thought of in detail before.

These sections at the end of each chapter have echoes of what a therapist would prompt you to think about, which is understandable as the author is a counsellor. I do believe that because the book was written by a counsellor who has experience on both sides of self-care, witnessing others struggles with the subject, it has given Karin more insight into the needs of other people regarding self-care.

Many other books are written with the author's experiences and could potentially not have the same wide area of reflection to prompt. The fact that Karin clearly labels each part of the reflection into "think," "feel," and "act" means that a reader can choose which parts of the reflection works best for them and skip to those bits.

The whole book is written with careful words and is laid out in such a way it would not scare off those who class themselves as not being readers. Other books can take a while to get to the point of the chapter, whereas this book is precise.

My overall feelings on the book are firstly, I would recommend it to anyone who is new to self-care as a starting platform. In addition, with the reflection aspect, it is original, and for a person new to the self-care ideology could replace the need for a therapist.

This could be hugely beneficial to someone who could not afford counselling.

On this note, it would be a good book for mental health teams and NHS counsellors (who only offer six sessions) to recommend to people so they can learn to take care of themselves. The impact of this book, if recommended like this, could be substantial.

—J.T.

This book is exactly what it says it is: different ways to integrate self-care into your daily life. It starts with an overview of why the author is writing about self-care, giving us an insight into her life.

Some introductions can be patronising, but this was not at all. There was no judgment, and Karin suggests that you know yourself best. The book covers twenty different self-care activities ranging from the usual spending time in nature and putting yourself first to ones we might not find obvious, such as personal space.

I liked that each topic starts with a quote that ties nicely into the chapter and the author uses her own personal experiences to explain each habit; this makes the book feel like you're speaking with a friend. The examples are easily relatable. For instance, in the putting your needs first chapter, the example of lending a friend money makes it easier to see how important your needs are when put into a perceptible example of money.

The layout of each chapter follows the same format, and this is something I particularly like a lot! The bullet points of how your life can improve with each habit are clear and concise, making it easy to digest.

I especially liked the reflection time section at the end of each chapter; it's almost like they've reached out a hand and brought you into the book. It gives you questions to help you reflect on your own personal circumstances and how each habit impacts your own life, as well as prompting you to make changes to improve your own self-care.

Whilst I would not normally read an eBook, the layout of this book was so easy to navigate and read on my phone.

I like the idea of the printable reminders and planners, which are a brilliant addition to this book!

Self-care is overlooked so much and isn't something I ever thought about until I started my training as a counsellor. This book makes it so easy to see the little ways in which you can look after yourself without too much effort. I would recommend this book to fellow counsellors, students, clients, and family members.

Overall, if you're looking for a proactive book to help work on your self-care, then this is the book for you!

—C.L.

20
SELF-CARE
HABITS

Develop Your Strengths, Use Your Resources,
Improve Your Life And Relationships

A Practical Guide To Setting Clear Boundaries
And Meeting Your Needs

KARIN BRAUNER

20 Self-Care Habits, 2ⁿᵈ Edition © 2021 by Karin Brauner.

All rights reserved.

Published by Author Academy Elite
PO Box 43, Powell, OH 43065

www.AuthorAcademyElite.com

Credit for quetzal image to natchapohn
(stock illustration ID: 609811654 Upload date: 29/09/2016)

LCCN: 2021905027

ISBN: 978-1-64746-746-3
ISBN: 978-1-64746-747-0
ISBN: 978-1-64746-748-7

Available in paperback, hardback, e-book

Other books by the author

The Beckoning Rooms
20 Self-Care Habits, 1ˢᵗ Edition

Yesterday I was clever, so I changed the world.
Today I am wise, so I am changing myself.

—*Rumi*

Table of Contents

Foreword
by Dr. Luis A. Recinos

Congratulations! You are about to embark on the wonderful journey towards self-discovery. It's not always an easy trip. It often is full of pitfalls, traps, tricks that the mind plays on us, memories and recollections of experiences we would prefer to forget and wish we never had, incredulity at times, as well as plenty of surprises, good and not so good ones.

Looking into the deepest aspects of ourselves has been compared by some with the task of peeling an onion. It's impossible to do it without shedding some tears once in a while. But at the end of the day, it is also a very positive undertaking. Once we become aware of the inappropriate thoughts, feelings, and behaviors that often had made our lives difficult, we can begin to abandon them and replace them with more appropriate ones.

Life isn't easy; that we know, and happiness often is quite elusive. Often we find that life is full of sorrow, guilt, resentment, depression, anxiety, confusion, fear, disappointments, anger, jealousy, rivalry, and so on—not a very nice picture. But it is also true that life can bring us much joy, pleasure, love, friendship, peace, satisfaction, success, and many feelings of accomplishment and fulfillment.

The book you are about to read will help you understand how and why many of the negative feelings, attitudes, and behaviors develop. It will give you the opportunity to explore those personal learning experiences that you may have had that eventually crystallized in the pessimistic side of things. But it will also give you the guidelines that will help you deal with some of the most common "slings and arrows of outrageous fortune" that usually lie behind the "sea of troubles" that tend to torment our soul.

You will learn that often, troubles arise because we have been taught not to put our needs first, but on the contrary, to put them last. In order to be likable and accepted by others, or maybe even to be loved by our parents, our needs and our interests have to go underground, where they are often forgotten. But eventually, they will demand our attention, but not before causing us much pain and anguish.

In this book, its author, Karin Brauner, starts by teaching us how to put our own needs first without falling into the trap of selfish narcissism. It is not an invitation to live the life of a rebellious child who wants to have his needs satisfied immediately. On the contrary, she aims at developing an attitude of a mature adult who will not fall into the trap of saying "yes" when, in fact, he wants to say "no," and who can say "no" when the situation so requires without feeling guilty, of course. She will guide you step by step to become aware of your own needs before saying "yes" to others, even though your "gut feelings" tell you it is not the best answer. In fact, she invites us to pay attention to those very poignant gut feelings that we all have but somehow tend to ignore. The organism has its own wisdom to guide us towards our own innermost truth, a truth that often tends to manifest itself precisely as a feeling "in the gut."

You will also learn the importance of planning ahead so you won't be taken by surprise and unprepared. Of course, uncertainty is quite common in life. But that doesn't mean we should not be capable of anticipating possibilities, both good and bad. You will also learn the importance of "limits." Indeed, many problems arise when we're unable to set our limits, both physical and emotional. As partners, employers, employees, friends, spouses, or parents, we have to have our limits clear. Otherwise, as Karin points out, we may fall into the trap of "enmeshment," a situation typical in dysfunctional relationships. From this, it follows the importance of being assertive, and the author will tell you how to accomplish this.

As you progress in your reading of the various chapters, you will learn how to discard negative thoughts about yourself and replace them with kindness. Of course, this seems to be quite obvious. But believe me, it's not as easy as it seems. How easy it is for us humans to learn how to belittle ourselves. But to be kind to ourselves? And that is why this chapter is particularly important because it will invite you to re-asses your self-worth and to stop being nasty to yourself. Also, you will learn about the futility of comparing yourself to others because, simply put, we are all unique and, therefore, it is senseless to engage in that sort of competition. But it seems that, as a result of our education, somehow we lose sight of that uniqueness and devote an enormous amount of energy trying to be that which we are not. In this book, you will learn how this happens and how to get over it and focus and develop your own sense of self.

And here is another interesting idea that Karin puts forth: "Stop doing," she says, "start being." Well, easier said than done, especially within the context of the contemporary worldview. But fortunately, she will explain how to achieve this goal. And throughout the book, she will give you, the reader, some practical guidelines to this end, as well as some reflection time to think, feel, and act upon the recently acquired discoveries about your *self*.

A Personal Note

Although the book is written from an apparently cognitive-behavioral perspective, as I progressed through my reading of the pages of the *20 Self-Care Habits*, I couldn't avoid establishing the relationship between many of the caring strategies proposed by the author with ideas advanced by some of the old masters. For example, the idea of *being* was put forth by Abraham Maslow in his *Towards a Psychology of Being*. From him, we can also rescue the notion of "peak experience," an example of which is superbly described by Karin in Chapter 13 when she discovered the value of solitude and all the beauty and truth contained in one single small flower. The value of being in nature and finding the "enchantment of everyday life" brought to mind the teachings of Thomas Moore. From this perspective, Karin's work is profoundly rooted in the best tradition of humanistic psychology, and, in my view, this gives her book an added value since it's these profoundly humanistic values that have been almost but completely lost in recent times, given the contemporary mores.

But life doesn't have to be centered only on *materialistic* points of view. The value of an individual doesn't depend, as an old acquaintance once stated, in terms of "how much he earns per year," or in terms of "how well adapted" he is to a maybe not very healthy social environment or interpersonal relationship, but rather in terms of his potential to become a fully functioning person.

A Final Comment

I strongly recommend the reader to pay attention to the epigraphs that open each chapter. They are very precious, and I commend Karin's for her good taste and judgment in selecting them. Also, notice the illustration of the little bird which appears in all the chapters. For those who may not know it, this is the national bird of Guatemala, Karin's country of origin. In Guatemala, it's known as the *Quetzal* (Pharomachrus Mocinno), and it represents liberty because it's a bird that dies when in captivity. What a marvelous allegory, since this book will help those courageous readers who have chosen to undertake the task of working through its various chapters, to free themselves from the chains of all those misguided thoughts, feelings, and behaviors that have kept them locked up in their own psychological prisons.

For an old teacher like myself, having the opportunity to write this foreword has been an honor, just like it was an honor to have Karin Brauner as a student many years ago at Francisco Marroquin University in Guatemala City when, as a young woman, she was just beginning her studies in psychology. Today, she is a fully-fledged professional in the area, contributing with her clinical work and writings to advance the well-being of her patients and followers.

I am sure that you will find the reading of this book quite a rewarding experience.

Guatemala, January 10, 2021

Foreword
by Andrea Musso, MA

When I met Karin, she was a student in the bachelor's program of Clinical Psychology in Guatemala. I remember her for her calm personality, dedication to her cases, and keen interest in learning to improve her practice without leaving aside her personal style as a therapist.

I was able to have her as a practitioner under my supervision. Karin worked following the curriculum and making assessments and reports for the cases she was accountable for in a proper manner and always on time. An exemplary practitioner. Remembering those times, Karin came to me additionally, respectful, in constant search for additional supervision for her cases, be these assessments or clients in later stages of their treatment. Her constant personal style marked by her calmness and right manners were a portrait of her own, as well as her soft smile. There were difficult times, which we find in everyone's life, and she was able to overcome them. Her personal history didn't interfere with her professional capability to be responsible for what corresponded to her.

Then, making assessments and reports. I consider that Karin responded well to the Cognitive Behavioural Therapy modality. She captured what she learned in lessons and traduced it into an integrative system marked by evaluation, diagnosis, and report according to protocol and clarity regarding treatment. The modality of play therapy in the case of children resulted in successful management, allowing Karin to get closer to the child from a position of empathy. Sitting down to discuss the cases with Karin was enriching. And it was way more enriching to see her unfold with a secure pace in her formation as a therapist.

Then, the trip. Karin had obtained a European passport and, to make the most of it, she decided to leave her comfort zone. A risky step is full of new experiences. Her wish to go to Europe was nothing new to her; this was already calling her in her existence. A very important step for her personal life with challenges of independence and change in social etiquette. At a professional level, to work in a new context, with a new means of communication (new language), with colleagues who had a different formation than hers, and with different teachers and supervisors. A whole professional adventure!

I want to express something that Karin points in her book, *20 Self-Care Habits*. Her life experience allowed her to generate and maximize strategies to maintain her own well-being. Being aware of how things unfolded in a new context in addition to the aforementioned experiences helped her develop assertive ways to put up boundaries, securing her assertiveness and management of emotions. From a professional perspective, theory in conjunction with practice. From a personal perspective, practice in conjunction with theory. I share the feeling of some therapists who consider being a therapist is a science and an art. Karin: science, study, effort, work; art: her persona, her capacity to empathize, and her serenity.

Life has its synchrony. My first child lives in London, United Kingdom. She's a psychologist. And for her to be connected with other Guatemalans, I gave her Karin's contact information. They both live far away but keep in touch. On one of my trips to visit my daughter and granddaughter, Karin invited us to spend the day in Brighton and Hove, where she lives. My excitement of seeing Karin was extreme! There we were, face to face, after many years. Karin, a professional and advanced author. Me, her ex-supervisor, and now her colleague. She gave us a tour around the place and then we went to eat something at a restaurant/pub. Ah, what a magical moment! Talks, nice food, some beer talks, and talks. Laughter, joy, and companionship. And another synchrony, she, who I use to supervise, is now a supervisor.

Few things we compare when one is academic, with the pleasure of seeing your pupil grow, develop assertively, and take steps with a personal seal. That's what I see in Karin. A whole person who knows how to evolve assertively in her personal and professional life. Sharing her knowledge with her readers. Her suggestions are assertive, clear, and applicable. Her readers can find in her book ways to self-care and ways of understanding what they think, feel, and behave. A cognitive behavioural approach is integrative to a phase of education, including the format selected for the text. The book contemplates self-care as well as caring for interpersonal relationships. I'm sure the readers will find this book fascinating. Additionally, readers can find Karin on social media, where she continues to offer help. To fully help the reader, a face-to-face appointment with Karin can also take place, and for sure, this will be a very enriching experience.

I hope I can see her soon and say to her face to face the words in this forward: I feel very proud to say that Karin was a student under my wings. Now, enjoy the book!

Preface to the 2nd Edition

Three years ago, I started writing a blog to inform, motivate, and encourage people online. It really changed how I worked and led me to develop an online presence and an online network of like-minded professionals and friends that remains to this day.

The first blog series I wrote was about self-care. As soon as I had finished it, I knew there was a book in there somehow.

I sat and planned. Lots of planning was involved in getting to the writing stages. Once the chapter titles were ready, I set out to find the right stories, quotes, and things to be gained from practising each habit.

I self-published that first edition, which is now replaced with a new and improved version. With the help of my publisher and the team, I've managed to make it even more than I ever expected.

As someone once told me, they understood why the first edition was written how it was: I am a very practical person, and the book reflects that. I was pleased with that. Getting awareness of who we are from others might not be the most important, but it does confirm that we're on the right track and being true to ourselves.

In this case, it confirmed that I was being genuine, congruent, and completely myself in my pursuit of helping others gain the insights about setting boundaries and meeting their needs.

I wanted people to gain those insights by learning from my mistakes, from my stories, from my journey. Some of it painful, but all of it helpful.

I don't fear self-disclosure. It makes me human, and I hope you can see that in this book. I chose the stories carefully to give you an idea of what you can achieve. We are human. We share similar trends. We might not have the same experiences, but we can relate. And that is what makes this book relatable and workable.

Setting clear boundaries sounds simple, but it can take time. It's not a one-stop-shop. It's a journey.

Learning to meet our needs in a world that tells us this is selfish is a hard one to crack—easier for some, harder for others. Once cracked, it opens a whole new realm of relating to ourselves and others—a realm where there's less resentment, more satisfaction, closer relationships, and so much more.

I hope to connect with you in one way or another—social media, my blog, coaching or counselling sessions, or by attending my online courses and workshops. Some are in development; some you'll see at the back of the book.

Introduction

The idea for this book came about from my journey of self-care. I took time getting to know what works for me and makes me happy, as well as what doesn't work for me and contributed to making me unhappy. I hope this book will help you find the same within your life and relationships.

It has been a steep learning curve.

My first attempt at setting boundaries was when I chose to move away from my home country. In this introduction, I won't go into the various reasons for my life-changing decision. I will say that I needed to do it to find myself and to start realising that some of the things I was doing were benefiting others but sometimes—most of the time—hindering my own life.

I wasn't putting my needs first, and neither were others. The benefits of this were temporary. A "thank you" was no longer enough.

But how does one start saying "no" or "not today" or "I'm busy taking care of myself" when one has become accustomed to being available for everyone at any time? How does one counteract the anger, disappointment, and even loss of relationships when trying to do the best for oneself?

Initially, dealing with the backlash of beginning self-care is a hard pill to swallow. It might be difficult to express your newfound boundaries and assertiveness and keep strong as people challenge them—and they will!

I promise you that the more you do it, the easier it gets.

The people who decide to stay while you strive to better look after yourself will benefit from this new you. You will become a person who sets boundaries and knows how to respect yourself and your feelings, making you more available to nurture those relationships in your life. Those who may have been angry or disappointed who left you during that season of transition might come back. It's possible no one will distance themselves at all! You could be setting an example for them, and they might be influenced by seeing how making self-care a priority has been beneficial to you.

What is self-care, and why is it relevant?

Based on what I have shared so far, I hope you have a basic idea of what self-care means. It's something that some many shy away from, as society often equates self-care to being "selfish" or not altruistic or compassionate to others' needs. Something that needs to be understood is that we are worthy of getting what we are giving to others!

Self-care is a way to maintain our well-being, our health, and our happiness. There isn't just one way to achieve it. There are many ways and several areas of our lives that require maintenance. It starts with the mind, body, spirit, and relationships.

The more we become aware of what we need and what makes us happy, the more we will pursue it. This is easier said than done. Upbringing and other life circumstances may not have led us to be able to execute self-care naturally. We may have been neglected, abandoned, or abused. We may have suffered a trauma that stunted our development or set us back in what we had already achieved within ourselves and our relationships.

Working through these issues is imperative to implement proper self-care. We must find ourselves worthy of being listened to, worthy of others respecting our boundaries and feelings, and worthy of equal, loving, and understanding relationships. If I must break it down to just a few words: worthy of happiness.

Self-care is relevant in our lives today. It is especially relevant in a world where instant gratification is king. A world where we can't wait for anything for fear of missing out or feeling entitled to something. A place where we put ourselves above others without considering how this affects them. We are constantly bombarded with communications and information.

We cannot undo the things that led up to this point in our lives. We can't remove things like technology. It's here to stay and is an essential part of our lives and businesses. We can't tell others how to think or feel or act, but we can start within ourselves. Small steps can make a massive difference!

Self-care can be incorporated in many different ways. Things such as going for a walk, finding a quiet spot to read, or enjoying your favourite drink are simple ways of exercising self-care. We must learn to spend time reflecting on what is important to us. Learning to honour our feelings and gaining respect through being assertive are other ways of exercising self-care.

Increasing your level of self-care leads to an improved life and better relationships. I believe that when you start to implement some—or all—the activities suggested, you will begin to reap the benefits of an improved life.

Structure of 20 Self-Care Habits

In this book, I want to provide the tools you will need to develop a habit in the areas of setting boundaries, honouring your feelings, learning to be on your own, and improving your relationships. In every topic, there will be a reflection relating to what is being discussed. I will explain what each item means and how your life and relationships can improve from practising these things. I also would like for you to spend some time in reflection. Spend time thinking, acknowledge how you are feeling, and performing actions that go along with what you have reflected upon.

I am not claiming to know everything or be the ultimate authority on self-care. I understand that the best person to know what will work best for you is indeed YOU. I have left space within the tools included for you to create your activity, thought, feeling, and reflection. I have also added a pretty, printable version of each topic so you can hang it in front of your desk, on your fridge, or wherever you will be able to see it and remember your self-care moments.

At the end of the book, there is a weekly and monthly planner to add the self-care activities you have found useful. I hope that through the suggested activities in this book, you will be able to develop your inner strengths, find your resources, and use them to improve your life and relationships.

How to use this book

There is no right or wrong way to use or read this book. I would suggest reading through the entire book to build a foundation for your self-care journey. Then, you can choose the suggestions that will work best for you and start implementing them at your leisure. You can also create your self-care activities and write them in the printables for each chapter—provided at the back of the book.

Don't forget to self-care

Today, I will remember to self-care by

Taking time to focus on my thoughts

Taking time to focus on my feelings

Doing something that's good for me

Get more specific and choose one of the activities in the book to focus on this week

CHAPTER ONE

Put Your Needs First before Saying Yes to Others

Very little is needed to make a happy life;
it is all within yourself, in your way of thinking.

—*Marcus Aurelius*

Marcus Aurelius makes a point that I can attest to. When I am at peace and happy within myself, everything else in my life goes well. This is reflected in the fact that my relationship with the person I've said "no" to is either left intact or improves because I've protected myself by saying "no."

For quite some time, I was the only one amongst my group of friends who had a car. People depended on me to drive them around. I was okay with this some of the time because we were usually going to the same place, and it wasn't out of my way to pick them up. One time, though, it was different. I had just arrived home from work and was ready to have a nap when I got a call from a colleague—one who was fully aware that I had just left work and was exhausted. I had even mentioned to them that I was planning to rest for the remainder of the day. She called me anyway. She wanted me to pick her up to take her to sort out some of her paperwork. I was fuming! She wasn't pleased when I said I wasn't going to get her straight away. In fact, I didn't get her at all.

I felt that this friend was looking out for herself and her needs only. I felt like she completely disregarded my needs.

If I had gone, I would have been even more tired as a result of not getting the rest I so urgently needed. I also would have been emotionally drained, resenting myself for not meeting my own needs. I realised from that point forward I would need to start saying no more often. I felt good lying in my bed, having the rest that I needed. Looking after myself was indeed the winner that day.

So, what does putting your needs first *really* mean? I believe it would be helpful if I rephrase the question: *What makes you happy?*

Putting your needs first will usually mean there's a choice to make, a choice between two or more activities—one more desirable, one you might want to avoid. One of these choices will either improve or keep your feelings toward yourself intact. Self-esteem, self-worth, well-being, and happiness will improve or remain the same. The other will impact a bit more negatively on these areas depending on the magnitude of the choices in question.

Consider this: A friend asks you to lend them £5. How likely are you to say yes or no? Now consider the same friend asks you to lend them the money, but this time they are asking for £1,000.

Which is more comfortable, lending £5 or £1,000? Is this friend reliable to pay either back? Would your friend understand if you said "no" to either amount? Will lending this amount of money prevent you from paying for something essential or put a dent in your savings? Would it stop you from enjoying Christmas, your holiday, or buying a new item that you wanted?

Reversely, is your self-respect, self-esteem, well-being, and happiness affected by the decision to say "yes" to lend either amount? How are these affected by you deciding to say "no"?

How will your life improve?

As you practice saying yes or no, it will get easier. It will become a part of who you are and how you live. You will develop a habit of looking after yourself.

Here is a brief list of how your life will improve:

❖ You will start to un-learn that "no" is a bad word.

❖ You will un-link saying "no" to being a bad person.

❖ You will recognise the benefits and positives in saying "no."

❖ You will start to value yourself more each time you choose to say "no."

❖ You will trust your gut and decide accordingly whether "yes" or "no" are best in each situation.

❖ You will only say yes when it's worth it and when you want to do something you are asked to do.

❖ You will feel more confident in your decisions and choices, improving your self-esteem and self-worth.

❖ You will be able to say "yes" to the things you want to do and the people you want to spend time with.

❖ You will have more time to yourself for self-care and growth.

How will your relationships improve?

❖ Your self-esteem and self-worth will depend on you and you alone—what others think of your "no" will not matter.

❖ Your confidence will grow in those who are there for you and value your needs.

❖ Your relationships will be more honest and equal.

❖ You will be able to say no without being guilt-tripped into changing your mind or feeling like you need to apologise.

❖ Your self-worth will not depend on how much you do for others.

Reflection Time

Think

❖ What do you need to consider when choosing between saying "yes" or "no"? I am a firm believer in trusting your instincts. What is your gut telling you?

❖ Is saying "yes" giving you a queasy, uneasy feeling?

❖ Is saying "no" making you feel insecure despite knowing that's how you would like to respond to this situation?

❖ Will your self-respect or self-esteem suffer from saying "yes" this time? Will your well-being and happiness suffer a result of saying "yes"?

Feel

❖ Position yourself in the now:

❖ What is going on within your body when it comes to choosing between yes or no?

❖ Position yourself in the future:

❖ What will the feeling be after committing to the yes or the no? Are you happy with the idea of that feeling?

Act

Make the decision that works best for you, considering the following questions:

- ❖ Does it positively affect your self-worth and self-esteem?
- ❖ Is it what you wanted to do?
- ❖ Did you trust your gut feeling?
- ❖ Does it make you happy?
- ❖ Did you put yourself first?

Self care moment for today

Put your needs first, before saying yes to others

**Very little is needed to make a happy life;
it is all within yourself, in your way of thinking.
- Marcus Aurelius**

think

Will your wellbeing and happiness suffer at any rate as a result of saying "yes"?

feel

What will the feeling be after committing to the yes or the no?

act

Make the decision that works best for you,

Add your own here:

think:

feel:

act:

CHAPTER TWO

Succeed When Tested: Plan Ahead

In preparing for battle I have always found that plans are useless, but planning is indispensable.

—Dwight D. Eisenhower

Although you may not be going into anything as catastrophic as a battle, it can certainly feel like an attack when people test your boundaries. The important thing is you have succeeded in starting your journey into assertiveness and self-care. Making the decision was the easy part. It is more complicated to be consistent and to get everyone around you on board. This "new you" might not be what others want. You will be able to say no, but it may not be acceptable to the person who has to hear it. You may have made time for yourself, but this might be perceived as odd or a sign of something being wrong with you.

When I shared in the previous chapter how I said no to my friend, I didn't mention that she resorted to begging and blackmail. From "But you are so nice, I will be forever your friend" to "This will upset me greatly if you don't help." I could have given in to the begging and blackmail, but the result would have been the failure to take care of myself. This would equal a setback in my goal of setting boundaries. I would have resented my friend and even myself for doing something against my better judgement.

Because I had the will to say no to the request, I did have my well-needed rest. I didn't resent myself, but I did find out what my friend was like and how far that relationship could go for me. Finally, I confirmed that my boundary was correct and indeed valid for me at this time, but it also allowed me to set even more limits, further improving my life and relationships.

Preparing for these challenges from friends and family means you will keep your boundaries and yourself safe. You will continue to have good relationships with friends and family but more importantly, and firstly, with yourself. This is where the challenge begins and why you need to plan ahead and be ready with an answer to those that might defy your need to look after yourself. You have to improve yourself and, eventually, your relationships.

How will your life improve?

❖   Every *defeat* will strengthen your ability to be
     more assertive.

❖   You will find it easier to set boundaries as you
     become consistent with executing them.

How will your relationships improve?

❖ Those with whom you practice your boundaries
   will begin to respect your boundaries and keep
   them.

❖ You will be more fulfilled in your relationships as
   both parties will know where the other stands.

❖ You will be able to discern better who your real
   friends are and decide how far each relationship
   will go.

Reflection Time

Think

❖ How much is your friendship or relationship worth to those close to you? Will they fall in line with your boundaries out of love for you, or will they put distance between you because they can't handle this new you?

❖ Would you respect your friends' boundaries when set? What would this mean for your relationship?

Feel

❖ Would it feel right to let a friend go because they are looking after themselves?

❖ Would it feel right to let go of someone who didn't respect the fact that you're looking after yourself?

Act

❖ Observe your friendships as you embark on this journey of setting boundaries.

❖ Challenge your friends when they don't honour your boundaries.

❖ Assess your relationships and manage them according to their respect and thoughtfulness for your needs.

❖ See what others near you are doing to look after themselves. How did they do it? How did they succeed? What did they do when challenged?

Self care moment for today

Succeed when tested – plan ahead

In preparing for battle I have always found that plans are useless, but planning is indispensable.
Dwight D. Eisenhower

think

Would you respect your friends' boundaries when set?

feel

Would it feel right to let a friend go because they are looking after

act

Challenge your friends when they don't honour your boundaries.

Add your own here:

think:

feel:

act:

CHAPTER THREE

Physical Boundaries: Personal Space

You're in my personal space, so get out of it.

—Carol Plum-Ucci

Are you like Carol, who finds her personal space incredibly valuable, or do you embrace it when people are around you in close proximity? I am a bit more like Carol in some respects. In my friendships, I know which friends I can invite to my home and which ones I'd instead meet at a café. The first group is better at keeping to social boundaries. They know that you don't stay for hours on end if you had a lunch date (the key is in the name of the activity) or ask to spend the night when I have said I am busy the next morning. The second group I meet outside of my home. My home is my safe space to go and be on my own. I can then enjoy the time spent together with this set of friends, as I know that we will be parting ways at some point. In this way, I have kept my physical boundaries safe.

I am closer to the friends in the first group than those in the second group, as we are more similar concerning physical and time boundaries. Also, we probably have more in common concerning life stories and experiences. This factor influences my decision on whether to invite to my home or to meet at a café.

Lastly, being in tune with myself and the history of my interactions with friends helps me make the decisions that will keep me safe—and sane! My self-esteem, happiness, and well-being will stay intact or improve, and I will have gathered even more evidence of how keeping my boundaries and staying true to myself makes a positive impact on myself and my relationships.

Personal space, therefore, refers to the distance between ourselves and others. It is the space in which we are comfortable interacting. We all have our limits, and some of us require more personal space than others. Keeping to our physical boundaries and having others hold to our needs of personal space impacts our emotional and psychological responses. If we feel someone is crossing our physical limits and not understanding our need for greater personal space, we might start to feel drained, angry, resentful, frustrated, and generally uncomfortable.

On the other hand, when someone is respectful of our physical boundaries and understands where we are comfortable, we will have a positive experience in that relationship.

Personal space is something that we take for granted as a society. Technology encroaches on our personal space every day through social media or via unsolicited phone calls. We sometimes have to share living quarters with people who might think differently about personal space.

Some of these things we can't help. Others, we can do something about—it's in our power to keep ourselves safe and happy.

How will your life improve?

❖ You can make the choices that will help you safeguard yourself from getting upset in your relationships.

❖ Keeping your personal space(s) like you want them to be, allows you to have places to go and "hide" when you feel like being on your own.

❖ You will feel happier with yourself for respecting your space and getting others to do the same.

How will your relationships improve?

❖ Being aware of what you need in a relationship concerning distance and personal space allows you to let others know what's okay and what isn't in your contact with them.

❖ You will be equipped with how to relate to certain friends and family—where to meet, how long to attend, and how to have your needs met and not walked over when in their presence.

Reflection Time

Think

❖ How would you define personal space?

❖ What does it mean to you to have physical boundaries?

Feel

❖ Remember a time where you felt drained and angry because your boundaries were not respected. Recreate that scene but this time, stick to your limits.

❖ How does this contrast to the original events?

Act

❖ Write down some steps to safeguard your personal space and physical boundaries.

❖ Write down some things you can do when your needs have been challenged regarding physical boundaries.

Self care moment for today

Physical Boundaries: Personal Space

You're in my personal space, so get out of it.

Carol Plum-Ucci

think

What does it mean to you to have physical boundaries kept and respected?

feel

How does it feel to have physical boundaries kept and respected?

act

Write down some steps to safeguard your personal space and physical boundaries.

Add your own here:

think:

feel:

act:

CHAPTER FOUR

There's a Time for Everything: Stop Doing, Start Being

To everything there is a season, and a time to every purpose under the heaven: A time to be born, and a time to die; a time to plant, and a time to pluck up that which is planted; a time to kill, and a time to heal; a time to break down, and a time to build up; a time to weep, and a time to laugh; a time to mourn, and a time to dance; a time to cast away stones, and a time to gather stones together; a time to embrace, and a time to refrain from embracing; a time to get, and a time to lose; a time to keep, and a time to cast away; a time to rend, and a time to sew; a time to keep silence, and a time to speak; a time to love, and a time to hate; a time of war, and a time of peace.

—*Ecclesiastes 3:1–8*

found this quote used in a blog post recently, and the author says this was the Bible's way of saying to everyone to "chill out." It made me chuckle, but I was nodding away because it's true. We are too busy doing that we forget to *be*.

When I started writing this book, I found it difficult to find the right time and place to do so. I would schedule writing time, but I would end up doing something else or just binging on Netflix! Afterwards, I would give myself a hard time for not having progressed with the book.

Through discussions with my peers in Facebook groups, I realised I wasn't on my own, while some were finding it easier to take time off their busy lives to look after themselves.

Writing is an art, and as artists in other areas will know—painting, sculpting, etc.—you have to pick your moments and go with the flow of the creative energies.

I have embraced the fact that some days—or weeks—I might not write anything, and others, I might write five or six chapters! I have welcomed the days of not doing much—or feeling like I haven't done much—because I need to look after myself and focus on other things like just being!

As the passage says, there is a time to do everything—a time to heal and a time to break down, a time to weep and a time to laugh.

In other words, there's a time to make or answer phone calls and a time to switch your phone off; there's a time to be on your own and a time to be with friends and family. The list goes on.

How will your life improve?

❖ You will be able to schedule time for "doing nothing" and free of responsibility without feeling guilty about it.

❖ You will have more time and energy for what you do need to do—when it's time to do it.

❖ You will be freed up to the idea that there is time for everything—there's time for being busy, and there's time for just "being."

How will your relationships improve?

❖ You will better manage your time to include being with your loved ones, but also have a healthy work/life balance.

❖ By setting time boundaries for yourself, you will be less inclined to stress about what you need to do because you have planned for it!

Reflection Time

Think

In the current climate, we are more likely to be running around, getting things done, being busy. But what happens when we burn out? Who is going to be the one doing all that running around and getting things done for us? Is it worth it to burn out, or can we allow ourselves some quiet, non-doing, non-busy time in our lives?

Will anything catastrophic happen if you allow yourself to just "be" for a period during the day?

Feel

Imagine yourself sitting down in your favourite spot. Maybe it's a sofa, under the shade of a tree, or a bench overlooking the sea. You have nowhere to go, nowhere to be, nothing to do. Take a few deep breaths and imagine how this feels. Is this something you can see yourself doing in your life, even if it is five to ten minutes a day to start?

Act

❖ Make a list of all the things you need to do in a day. Separate them into two different groups. One is a list of priority items, and the other, a list of items that are not a priority.

❖ Plan how you are going to achieve them without missing out on tea breaks, lunch breaks, rest breaks from the computer, or a focused task.

❖ Plan time during the day when you can start having your five to ten minutes of "being." Build this up as you become accustomed to taking these breaks.

Self care moment for today

Stop doing, start being
To everything there is a season, and a time to every purpose under the heaven
Ecclesiastes 3:1-8

think

Will anything go wrong happen if you allow yourself to just "be" for a moment in the day?

feel

How does it feel to sit down and do nothing for 5-10 minutes?

act

Schedule and build up your "being" time each day.

Add your own here:

think:

feel:

act:

CHAPTER FIVE

—

Emotional Boundaries

Daring to set boundaries is about having the courage to love ourselves, even when we risk disappointing others.

—Brené Brown

loved this quote as soon as I saw it. If you love yourself, you will be well. Disappointing others will happen one way or another, but setting boundaries that make you feel safe and happy are essential to your emotional well-being. If the relationship is strong enough, it will survive your assertiveness.

Having emotional boundaries requires you to be assertive with others to encourage love and respect in relationships. These boundaries keep your relationships healthy and well.

Just like physical boundaries, emotional boundaries help keep you safe. When you are being loved and respected, you will feel comfortable and have a positive relationship with that person. On the other hand, if someone crosses your emotional boundaries, you might feel angry, exhausted, and uncomfortable with them.

Setting emotional boundaries means that you keep yourself safe from so many things:

❖ Manipulation from others.

❖ Enmeshment—losing yourself in a relationship to the point that you forget who you are.

❖ Being pushed into situations that make you feel uncomfortable or could cause emotional harm.

How will your life improve?

❖ The way you see yourself will be more positive as your identity remains intact.

❖ Your self-worth will be high, and others will acknowledge this.

❖ You will be the real "you" without guilt or shame.

❖ Your emotional needs will be met.

❖ You will know you are responsible for your happiness, not anyone else's, and you can live this truth without feeling guilty.

How will your relationships improve?

❖ It will become easier to discern who you can get close to and who to keep at a bit of a distance.

❖ You will be mindful of how others treat you and whether they respect your boundaries.

❖ You will learn to respect yourself by keeping your emotional boundaries, as well as become an example to others on how to respect themselves and maintain their own boundaries.

Reflection Time

Think

❖ Have you ever been in a situation where you were not sure of your identity? Did you question what you were meant to do or how you were expected to act? Did you doubt yourself and your boundaries, resulting in your agreement with doing something that made you feel uncomfortable?

❖ If you could go back to that day, how would you set boundaries so that you didn't find yourself feeling uncomfortable or possibly upset with yourself for not speaking up?

❖ How would you keep yourself safe from emotional upset and forfeiting on your own boundaries?

Feel

❖ How does it feel to be able to speak up and say, "Actually, I don't think to do A or B is for me, but you go ahead!"

Act

❖ Write a list of what makes you feel emotionally safe and within your boundaries.

❖ Write a list of what doesn't make you feel emotionally safe or within your boundaries.

❖ Keep an eye out for these things in your life and speak up when you start to feel unsafe.

Self care moment for today

Emotional Boundaries

Daring to set boundaries is about having the courage to love ourselves, even when we risk disappointing others. -- Brene Brown

think

How would you keep yourself safe from emotional upset and forfeiting on your own boundaries?

feel

How does it feel to stick to your boundaries?

act

Write a list of what makes you feel emotionally safe and within your boundaries.

Add your own here:

think:

feel:

act:

CHAPTER SIX

Be Assertive and Follow Through

Staying silent is like a slow growing cancer to the soul and a trait of a true coward. There is nothing intelligent about not standing up for yourself. You may not win every battle. However, everyone will at least know what you stood for—YOU.

—Shannon L. Alder

"**I**f I knew then what I know now..."

Oh, I can't count the number of times I kept quiet or the number of times I wasn't assertive when someone said something hurtful or challenged who I was! I would only get angrier and unhappy with myself every time I knew what to say, but the words just wouldn't come out.

As time went by and I started practising the things I am now writing about, I felt less angry and unhappy with myself. I became confident in who I am and accepted that this is okay and quite great!

It took some practice to get good at it. Sometimes I don't "win," as the quote says, but I still feel better about myself, and I am more confident in what I say and do when it comes to keeping my boundaries and being assertive.

Being assertive is a huge part of setting boundaries. As Shannon says in the quote above, everyone will know what you stood for. If you stand up for yourself, you are not harming anyone; you are only helping yourself when relating to others. You are promoting your relationships to be the best they can be.

Being open and honest and using "I" statements are two ways in which you can practice being assertive. Being open and honest is critical because it will encourage you to talk and state what is okay for you and what isn't. This also gives you the opportunity to express your expectations of the person to whom you are speaking.

By using "I" statements, you are not blaming others. Notice the difference between these two statements:

- "I felt that you weren't listening to what I was saying."

- "You never listen to what I'm saying."

You shift the focus from the other person to yourself.

The worst thing you can do to yourself—or one of them anyway—is to get upset in a situation where you have the power to stick to your boundaries.

How will your life improve?

❖ You will get progressively better at setting boundaries, resulting in you being happy with yourself
and within yourself.

❖ You will know where you stand as well as make
a stand when you need to.

❖ You will be less likely to resent yourself for not
speaking up.

How will your relationships improve?

❖ Those around you will know what buttons not to
push with you, and likewise, you will learn what
buttons not to push with them.

❖ Healthy communication, as well as open and
honest dialogue, will become a standard in your
relationships. This will minimise arguments
because "I" statements help dissipate the blaming
and guilt-tripping games.

Reflection Time

Think

What is the worst thing that can happen when you are assertive with someone?

Feel

Imagine yourself in a situation when you want to be on your own, but you are being pressured to hang out with someone. Consider the two statements:

- ❖ I feel that my need for space is not being respected right now.

- ❖ Ok, let's spend some time together.

Which one feels better?

Act

Write down an action plan for a situation where you could either keep quiet and struggle within yourself or be assertive and feel happier with yourself. Write down how you will be assertive and avoid the emotional upset.

Self care moment for today

Be assertive and follow through

"There is nothing intelligent about not standing up for yourself...everyone will at least know what you stood for—you."

—Shannon L. Alder

think

What is the worst thing that can happen when you are assertive with someone?

feel

Assess whether it feels better to say yes or no to someone today.

act

Act on your assessment. Say yes or no assertively and confidently

Add your own here:

think:

feel:

act:

CHAPTER SEVEN

Trust Your Gut Feelings: Listen To Yourself

Never discredit your gut instinct. You're not paranoid. Your body can pick up vibrations, some better than others, and if something deep inside you says something's not right about a person or situation, trust it and keep it pushing.

—Anonymous

A s a counsellor, trusting my instincts and intuition is something I've developed from the start of my training. I wouldn't work without it. There are unconscious nuances that are communicated between two people, which are enhanced in the therapeutic relationship.

Trusting my instincts helps me be a better therapist and, in turn, better help my clients. This also crosses over to my personal life and relationships, as I learn to keep my boundaries and be assertive, as well as honouring my feelings.

The vibrations mentioned in the quote are those unconscious nuances I mentioned above. They could be a vibe sent from someone of whose presence you're in. You may sense that they don't like you as a result of them saying something that feels passive-aggressive. Another example could be if you are being asked to join in on an activity that doesn't sit well with you. The situation reminds you of something that happened in your past that didn't end well, and it ultimately triggers your feelings of moving away.

What happens if you stay in that person's company or do that activity or ignore the memory of that adverse situation from your past? You might end up resenting yourself for not following what you knew was the right thing to do—stop being friends with that person, say no thanks to that activity, or move away from that situation since you already have a feeling how it might end.

How will your life improve?

❖ As you practise trusting your gut feelings, you get better at setting boundaries.

❖ You will become more efficient at recognising situations that might upset you or disturb your peace.

❖ You will become more consistent at trusting your instincts as well as taking heed to your gut feelings as they occur.

How will your relationships improve?

❖ You will develop relationships that fulfil you and with those who respect your boundaries, honour your feelings, as well as who you are as a person.

❖ You will be more selective about who you allow into your life and how close or distant you are with each of your acquaintances, friendships, and family members.

❖ Trusting your gut feeling will lead you to improve your communication about what you feel is right for you and what is not.

Reflection Time

Think

Think of a time when your gut feelings were so overwhelming, and you knew you had to act but didn't. What did you feel after ignoring that overwhelming feeling? What would you do now, knowing the outcome could have been different if you had taken heed to those gut feelings?

Feel

Imagine yourself doing something different in that situation now.

❖ You stop doing an activity you didn't want to do in the first place.

❖ You move away from that person.

❖ You say no to that situation or person.

How does that feel? What is the difference between how you feel now and how you felt at the time that you failed to act?

Act

Write down a list of past experiences you didn't enjoy and wish you had refrained from participating. Keep this list in mind when making plans with others, whether you are invited or are planning your own.

20 Self-Care Habits

Self care moment for today

Trust your gut feelings:
Listen to yourself

Never discredit your gut instinct. Your body can pick up vibrations, some better than others,

Anonymous

think

How can you do something different when your gut tells you something is not right?

feel

How does it feel to take action when your gut tells you to?

act

Practice listening to your inner voice, to your gut, and acting on what feels better for you to do in that moment.

Add your own here:

think:

feel:

act:

43

Challenge Negative Thoughts and Feelings about Yourself and Replace Them with Kindness

Only allow yourself to think negative thoughts and/or complain about anything for three minutes, three times a day.

—Karen Salmansohn

appreciate this quote. Give yourself time to complain but minimise it to three minutes a day, three times a day. It is important to acknowledge those feelings and thoughts that aren't positive because when we don't, they usually resurface and sometimes get more intense.

Give yourself three minutes or ten; whatever time works for you. Allow yourself to sulk, be moody, or be upset about whatever it is that you're dealing with. Give those emotions and thoughts the airtime they deserve, but make it brief. Replace them with good and positive ones to maintain your peace and ability to move forward.

Challenging your negative thoughts and feelings equates to not allowing yourself to be stuck:

❖ Meditating on things that don't contribute to having a healthy and positive thought life.

❖ Believing things about yourself and your life that are not true.

Taking the time to work through those negative thoughts and feelings will help you to come to terms with how they came about and encourage you to learn how to deal with the issues that they stem from in positive ways.

How will your life improve?

❖ You will be able to differentiate between those thoughts that are true and those that are false.

❖ You will be able to give space and time to those emotions and thoughts that don't benefit you, and in turn, give that space back to more worthwhile and positive thoughts and feelings about yourself.

How will your relationships improve?

❖ You will process your emotions and thoughts in such a way that you will be able to:

- Communicate more openly about those things that harm you

- Regroup after a falling-out and repair the relationship in a more effective and productive way

Reflection Time

Think

We have hundreds, if not thousands, of thoughts in a day. Some may be truthful and others hurtful. What you decide to do with these thoughts is what determines your perspective about yourself and your life.

How much truth is there to the thoughts and feelings you have about yourself?

Feel

Recall how it felt when you had a dreadful day, and everything you did seemed to be the wrong thing. What thoughts did you have, and how did they make you feel?

Now replace them with positive and kind thoughts about yourself. How is that day different in your eyes?

Act

Search for or create positive affirmations. Meditate on them and speak them to yourself when it feels like negative thoughts are taking over your life.

Self care moment for today

Challenge negative thoughts and feelings about yourself and replace them with kindness

Only allow yourself to think negative thoughts and/or complain about anything for three minutes, three times a day. - Karen Salmansohn

think

How much truth is there to the thoughts and feelings you have about yourself?

feel

Say something nice to yourself and notice how you feel.

act

Replace negative thoughts for positive and kind thoughts about yourself

Add your own here:

think:

feel:

act:

CHAPTER NINE

Attend a Support Group

*I am building a healthy support system and
learning to use it readily.*

—Maureen Brady

A support group is a space where people with the same issues, problems, or ideas get together to share their experiences and even solutions they might have. This one might not be for everyone. Luckily, we live in a day and age where "attending" doesn't mean in person. It can be on Facebook or other social media platforms. I am a part of a few groups for a variety of things. It's just nice to write a post in one of these groups and see that I'm not the only one struggling with that issue! Knowing there are others out there who struggle with similar things reassures us that we are not alone.

Sharing is caring, they say. I believe this to be true. If we share our worries and pain, it usually helps us cope with it and get through it. Whether you do join a support group or not, have a support system in place. It could be family, friends, or others who think or share minds with you. There are people who you can ultimately go-to for a rant, a cry, or a laugh.

How will your life improve?

❖ You will know that you are not alone.

❖ You will know that others understand what you are going through.

How will your relationships improve?

❖ You will be able to share your experience and help others going through similar things.

❖ You can build new friendships and increase your support system with like-minded people.

❖ Your other relationships can remain the same, knowing that you have somewhere to talk about things they might not understand.

Reflection Time

Think

❖ Have you ever considered joining a support group? Are you a part of any support groups online?

❖ What makes you feel safe in a group setting? What stops you from joining one?

Feel

❖ How does it feel to know that there might be a group of people out there that understand exactly how you feel?

Act

❖ Research online support groups. Join and start a conversation. Do it anonymously if you feel it is necessary.

❖ Attend a local support group to see what it's about. Determine whether it's something in which you would like to participate.

20 Self-Care Habits

Self care moment for today

Attend a Support Group

"I am building a healthy support system and learning to use it readily."
— Maureen Brady

think

What would make you feel safe in a support group setting?

feel

How does it feel to know that there might be a group of people out there that understand

act

Visit a group and see if it's something you want to be a part of.

Add your own here:

think:

feel:

act:

CHAPTER TEN

Stop Comparing Yourself to Others

*Stop thinking you're doing it all wrong. Your
path doesn't look like anybody else's because
it can't, it shouldn't, and it won't.*

—Eleanor Brownn

Uniqueness lies in not comparing oneself to others.

—Raheel Farooq

Have you ever cringed at hearing a parent or a teacher tell a child that they should be like someone else? Has someone ever said that to you? Oh, it makes my stomach turn a bit, just thinking about the damage that does to someone! Why do I have to be like him or her? Why can't I be myself and that be good enough and even awesome enough? The truth is, I can, and I should believe it is so.

You are good enough as you are now. Of course, there is always room to evolve and develop. So your present self will be better in some ways than who you were yesterday. Doesn't comparing yourself to yourself feel better already?

When you compare yourself to others, you are cheating yourself out of the greatness that you have to offer to yourself and others! When we start looking at other's clothes, job, partner, hair, etc., and compare it to our own, we sometimes look at ourselves like we are lacking.

You are unique. You are great just the way you are. Do not allow yourself or others to tell you otherwise. Your path, as the quote above says, is your own.

As we have spoken about in other chapters, honour your feelings and instincts. Do what feels right for you! This includes not comparing yourself to others. That will bring you down and make you forget the great things you have to offer.

How will your life improve?

❖ You will be free to be yourself, no matter what.

❖ Your self-esteem and self-confidence will be higher, as you will know that you are good enough, just as you are.

How will your relationships improve?

❖ You won't need to act or try to be someone different or someone you think others want or expect you to be.

❖ You will set boundaries that will prevent yourself and other people from comparing you to others.

❖ By accepting yourself as you are, others will do the same.

Reflection Time

Think

- ❖ Think back to your past and whether your parents compared you to others.

- ❖ Currently, do the people in your life compare you to others?

- ❖ Do you consistently catch yourself comparing yourself to others? What does this do to you? What feelings and thoughts does it bring up?

Feel

- ❖ Allow yourself to experience any emotions that come up as you remember being compared to others. Give yourself five minutes to feel them.

- ❖ Now give yourself five minutes to feel what it is like to let go of those comparisons and put a stop to them.

Act

- ❖ Visualisation: Go back to the past and tell your parents, teachers, and yourself you are good enough, and you are going to be yourself from now on, no matter what they thought of you in the past.

- ❖ Tell someone in your current life the same thing.

❖ Catch yourself when you start comparing yourself to others and regroup, put new thoughts in its place, ones that let you know that you don't need to be anyone else other than who you are.

20 Self-Care Habits

Self care moment for today

Stop comparing yourself to others

"Your path doesn't look like anybody else's because it can't, it shouldn't, and it won't."
— Eleanor Brown

think

Do you or other people compare you to others? how can you change this?

feel

Give yourself five minutes to feel what it is like to let go of those comparisons and put a stop to them.

act

Go back to the past and tell youreveryone that you are good enough.

Add your own here:

think:

feel:

act:

CHAPTER ELEVEN

—

Work Through Past Expectations: Find a New Way That Works for You

I have learned that as long as I hold fast to my beliefs and values—and follow my own moral compass—then the only expectations I need to live up to are my own.

—Michelle Obama

We are expected to know what we will do with the rest of our lives when we are just figuring out what life means. Not all expectations are this big, and this is where the problems arise.

Expectations, both big and small, pose a threat to your well-being and being true to yourself. We are stressed and pressured to achieve and become what others believe we should become. Some of us do this to the point of sacrificing a happy life for a pat on the back from significant people in our lives.

Others' expectations of you and how you live your life can be damaging. Having said that, it depends on how they are phrased or expressed. If you are being encouraged to be the best you can be, without specifics of what that looks like, that's positive. But if you are told that you have to be a certain way to be successful, that is a negative pressure that will hinder you instead of helping you.

Take the time to reassess what's important to you and you alone. Think about how you live your life and what makes it yours. Doing this will free you from the need to please others or help you shut out all those expectations and imperatives that society dictates to us. Most people have their idea of what it is to have a happy life. Live your own life free from others' expectations.

How will your life improve?

❖ Your boundaries will get stronger and stronger as you challenge others' thoughts on how your life *should* look.

❖ You will be able to make choices that make sense to you, with little to no outside influence.

    o Note: Although outside influence might be minimal or none at all, you can allow others to suggest and advise, but in the end, it's your decision to make.

How will your relationships improve?

❖ You will be freed from the pressure and stress of meeting others' expectations, decreasing the possibility of feelings of resentment for their input.

❖ You will become skilled at voicing your needs and preferences, which will encourage others to respect your boundaries and your way of life.

Reflection Time

Dealing with life—both externally (other people, situations, influences) and internally (thoughts, feelings) is a learning curve. The process of learning to navigate through life using our strengths and resources is essential. Possessing those strengths and resources means that we can decide what to do with ourselves or which path to take. Once we are no longer children, we don't need someone there to tell us every step. Developing autonomy and independence is something that needs to be encouraged so we can function well when our parents can no longer be there for us.

Think

❖ Which decisions in your life have worked out well? What has caused it to work well? How did others influence your decision that worked well? Did you feel pressured into making this decision? Did you make it because you wanted to or because someone expected you to? Have others dictated it, or have you challenged it and moved yourself to where you want to be?

Feel

❖ Think of a situation where you did something without thinking or considering anyone's expectations of you. How did that feel?

❖ How would it feel to make more decisions without the shadow of someone else's opinion, input, or expectation?

Act

❖ Reassess and review what decisions you have made in life that are working for you and making you happy. Think about how others' expectations have influenced them.

❖ Consider the level of influence from others that you would consider acceptable when you make life decisions.

20 Self-Care Habits

Self care moment for today

Work through past expectations

I have learned that as long as I hold fast to my beliefs and values then the only expectations I need to live up to are my own. — Michelle Obama

think

Do others have a great impact in the decisions you make for your life?

feel

How would it feel to make more decisions without the shadow of someone else's expectations?

act

Consider the level of influence from others that you would consider acceptable when you make life decisions.

Add your own here:

think:

feel:

act:

—

CHAPTER TWELVE

Sit with Your Feelings, No Matter How Difficult

Nothing in life is to be feared, it is only to be understood.

—Marie Curie

Does sitting with difficult feelings sound a bit counter-productive? Well, in fact, it is the best thing you can do with any feelings that you experience. As Marie Curie says in this quote, understanding is critical. Taking the time to understand what is going on for us is the best thing we can do to move forward.

I see this with people I meet in my line work. Anger is the most difficult emotion to contend with, sit with, and work through. It scares people because they might feel like they will lose control or not be able to come back from it in one piece. Resentment and guilt are others. Once you start to look at what each emotion is and how it is affecting your life, you can start working on them. Is the emotion a survival strategy that used to work but has now stopped working? Is it a feeling that is making relationships difficult? It is imperative to work through these things and free yourself from the shackles that unprocessed feelings might cause you to endure.

Negative feelings can pop up at the most inopportune time. Sometimes, all we want to do is hide away, sleep, and hope these problematic feelings go away. Struggling with difficult feelings and emotions is all part of being human. You don't have to fight on your own. Reach out to support groups, a therapist, or a friend. Get support while you figure out what your feelings are telling you and how you will resolve the situations or relationships from which they arose.

How will your life improve?

❖ You will be free from the intensity of past unre-solved emotions.

❖ You will be able to recognise when you might need to sit with painful feelings and work through them to move forward. This point will be reinforced in another chapter.

❖ Your coping mechanisms with painful feelings will be healthier, and you will be able to deal with them more effectively, with less fear or trepidation.

How will your relationships improve?

❖ Forgiveness, compassion, and understanding of yourself will lead you to forgive, understand, and be compassionate with others.

❖ Dealing with those past hurts and moving forward from them will cultivate a better relationship with those who wronged you.

❖ You will be able to work through things as they happen, rather than leaving them to be dealt with at a future time when they will feel even more overwhelming.

Reflection Time

When you process your feelings and even befriend them for a little while, you are better off in the long term.

Think

❖ Recall a time when you or someone you know was going through a hard time. What did you or the person do? Did you/they sit with it? Did you/they process it?

Feel

❖ Find a feeling that you find difficult to process, whether it's directed towards yourself or not. If you have hidden it or avoided it in the past, try something new—sit with it. If it feels like too much to do this, stop here and get a therapist to help you.

❖ Allow yourself to experience the emotion entirely. Is it overwhelming, or can you manage it? You can? Great! Work through it and all the thoughts and other feelings it brings up. How does it feel to have done this? Freer? Lighter?

Act

❖ Next time you find yourself dealing with complicated feelings, stop and let them be. Allow time to regroup and think about them. Work through them, let them go, then move forward with your life.

Self care moment for today

Sit with your feelings, no matter how difficult

"Nothing in life is to be feared. It is only to be understood." – Marie Curie

think

Recall a time where you dealt with difficult feelings. How did you get through it?

feel

Allow yourself to feel something difficult and see how well you manage i

act

Allow time to regroup and think about difficult feelings.

Add your own here:

think:

feel:

act:

CHAPTER THIRTEEN

Mental Benefits of Being in Nature

*Just living is not enough... one must have sunshine,
freedom, and a little flower.*

—Hans Christian Andersen

recently attended an ecotherapy seminar. Ecotherapy is a type of therapy where the sessions take place somewhere in nature. The seminar I attended took place in a wooded area. The course leader put a table and chairs in the middle of our meeting area, so we still had that seminar feel, but we were completely immersed in nature.

For one of the exercises, we went exploring and had to choose something to look at. We were told not to think about it too much but to find something that we found particularly interesting. I walked a few feet away from where we were. I was feeling cold, so I wanted sunshine. I found a little tree stump and sat there for the duration of the activity. I started looking around but wasn't interested in the bigger picture. Instead, I focused on some tiny yellow flowers that were near me.

I lost myself in them.

It reminds me of the quote above. At that moment, I needed that little flower and that bee that came to visit. Losing myself in seeing the flower meant that all my thoughts were gone, even if just for those few moments. I had a break from stress…from everyday problems.

I could just *be*.

Spending time in nature is more relevant and meaningful than we might realise.

As I found out during my seminar experience, spending time in nature will help you refocus and regroup when stressed or worried. It could also serve as just a quiet time for yourself for no other reason than just *being*.

We have many responsibilities in our lives. We are rushing to get here and there and get everything done. It is easy to get stressed, anxious, depressed, and too busy to make time for ourselves.

Spending time in nature doesn't have to take hours of your time. You could take ten minutes a day to spend outside—if you have a garden, that makes it even easier. If you don't, there might be a park near you or a wooded area to go sit down for a while. It could become a meditation space that you might want to explore.

How will your life improve?

❖ You will reduce stress and its effects on your life.

❖ Your mood will improve from repeatedly seeing beautiful things and taking the time to focus on them.

❖ Spending time in nature might allow for that self-care time that is so difficult to schedule into your busy life.

How will your relationships improve?

❖ Your home life will be affected, as you will be relaxed and better able to engage with your loved ones.

❖ If your mood is better and you feel better about yourself, you'll feel better when relating to those around you.

❖ Including friends and family in your activities in nature can positively influence their lives.

Reflection Time

Think

❖ When was the last time you spent time in nature? What did you get out of it?

Feel

❖ Close your eyes and imagine yourself being in the middle of a forest (or take yourself to a nature site and do this whilst you are there). You are sitting on the grass. How does it feel on your hands? Touch the trees and flowers near you. How do they feel? Is the sun shining? How does it feel on your face and arms? Sometimes looking at the sky is lovely. The colours and shapes of the clouds are fantastic to see.

Act

❖ Schedule five to ten minutes every day to spend time in nature. This could be a walk in the park or just focusing on your office plant for that time if you can't get away. Make this a priority and chart the effects of spending that time concentrating on nature and nothing else.

Self care moment for today

Mental benefits of being in nature

Just living is not enough... one must have sunshine, freedom, and a little flower.
—Hans Christian Andersen

think

When was the last time you spent time in nature?

feel

Go outdoors and find a peaceful place to experience it fully.

act

Schedule 5-10 minutes every day to spend time in nature

Add your own here:

think:

feel:

act:

CHAPTER FOURTEEN

—

Physical Benefits of Being in Nature

A walk in nature is a perfect backdrop to combine exercise, prayer, and meditation while enhancing the benefit of these activities.

—Chuck Norris

As mentioned in the quote, nature can give us a variety of mental and physical benefits. An article by PLOS ONE[1] addresses both the mental and physical benefits of being in nature. Being in nature can help us mentally by improving our mood, decreasing anxiety and depression symptoms, and increasing happiness and mindfulness. Here are a few of the physical benefits found in the study:

- ❖ Reduction of hypertension

- ❖ Reduction of respiratory tract and cardiovascular illnesses

- ❖ Restored attention

- ❖ Reduced mental and physical fatigue

Spending time in nature will help your physical health as much as your mental health. In fact, you can combine both. They go hand in hand. Whether you are walking to the park, the woods, or the beach, you are exercising. You are also stimulating your other senses and when you take in the views. All of these allow your mind to relax and focus on the beauty before you.

---

[1] Richardson M, Cormack A, McRobert L, Underhill R, "30 Days Wild: Development and Evaluation of a Large-Scale Nature Engagement Campaign to Improve Well-Being," *PLoS ONE*, 11(2): e0149777. doi.org/10.1371/journal.pone.0149777

How will your life improve?

❖ By consistently spending time in nature, you will be more active physically, which improves your overall health.

How will your relationships improve?

❖ You will recharge your social batteries and be more engaged when you meet with friends and family.

Reflection Time

Think

❖ How long do you spend in nature every week? How easy would it be to add 5–10 minutes a day to your schedule for spending time in nature? If it is difficult, think about why that is and how you can change that.

Feel

❖ Feel what it's like to be indoors. Are you getting enough fresh air? Maybe it's still too cold to have the windows open. Is the heating on? This might be impacting your health, and a bit of fresh air might be just what you need to carry on working. Go out and feel the air on your face, the sunshine, or the cold breeze. How different does that feel from being indoors?

Act

❖ Research some areas near your home and work where you could go on your time off or during your lunch break. Try to do this once a week and keep adding days to it until it becomes second nature.

Self care moment for today

Physical benefits of being in nature

A walk in nature is a perfect backdrop to combine exercise, prayer, and meditation while enhancing the benefit of these activities. -Chuck Norris

think

How easy would it be to add 5-10 minutes a day to your schedule for spending time in nature?

feel

Go out and feel the air on your face, the sunshine or the cold

act

Make a list of some areas near you to spend some time each day.

Add your own here:

think:

feel:

act:

CHAPTER FIFTEEN

Mixing Exercise and Nature: The Facts

*Human bodies are designed for regular physical activity.
The sedentary nature of much of modern life probably
plays a significant role in the epidemic incidence of
depression today. Many studies show that depressed
patients who stick to a regimen of aerobic exercise
improve as much as those treated with medication.*

—Andrew Weil

Regular physical activity impacts positively on our mind and body. Consistent physical activity in nature will help reduce the levels of depression, anxiety, and stress in our lives.

Because of the advancement of technology, we have apps that can remind you to reach your goals for physical activity. I have one that tracks my steps and even captures data about how long I've walked and the benefits I gained from it. It informs me of how much I've got left to reach my daily goals.

One of the advantages of these apps is that it gives us statistics about our exercise and movement. Just like the apps, there is research that tells us, in numbers, how important it is to exercise and spend time in nature.

Here are some statistics of what will improve when mixing exercise with nature[2]:

How will your life improve?

❖ Improves short-term memory by 20%

❖ Restores mental energy by looking at pictures of nature or being in nature itself. This can elicit feelings of awe and, therefore, a mental energy boost.

❖ Lowers stress by lowering cortisol levels

❖ Lower levels of inflammation and hypertension symptoms

❖ Reduces the risk of developing myopia

❖ Increase concentration

❖ Sharper thinking and creativity

❖ Possible anti-cancer effects

❖ Improved mental and immune system health

❖ Longer life span

---

[2] Lauren F Friedman and Kevin Loria, "11 scientific reasons you should be spending more time outside," *Business Insider, April 22, 2016.* uk.businessinsider.com/scientific-benefits-of-nature-outdoors-2016-4?r=US&IR=T

How will your relationships improve?

❖ Share these lovely experiences with your loved ones and see the effects in yourself and your relationships.

Reflection Time

Think

❖ Are there any of the benefits in the list above something you'd like to see more of in your life?

Feel

❖ How would it feel to be able to achieve one or two of the personal improvements mentioned above, from just 20–30 minutes of exercise in nature as described above?

Act

❖ Make a list of goals you want to achieve and how you want to reach them, then implement them one by one.

20 Self-Care Habits

Self care moment for today

Mixing Exercise and Nature

Human bodies are designed for regular physical activity. — Andrew Weil

think

what benefits of mixing exercise and nature would you like to see more of in your life?

feel

How would it feel to start seeing the effect of these benefits?

act

Make a list of goals you want to achieve and how you want to reach them.

Add your own here:

think:

feel:

act:

CHAPTER SIXTEEN

Find Clarity, Promote Creativity: Quiet and Solitude Is Important

Solitude is creativity's best friend, and solitude is refreshment for our souls.

—Naomi Judd

In solitude the mind gains strength and learns to lean upon itself.

—Laurence Sterne

Talking about being in nature in the last few chapters relates well to quietness and solitude. Yes, we can be in nature with friends and family, but where we might get the most benefit is being quiet within nature. There is time to do both.

In solitude—not the same as being lonely—is where we can find our creativity and clarity in our current life issues and situations. It is such a powerful thing to do for ourselves, and in turn, it will benefit our relationships. Find that space to regroup and replenish your mind, soul, and body.

Quiet and solitude is where we refresh our souls or regain our mind's strength, as indicated in the quotes above.

How will your life improve?

❖ Your creativity will improve.

❖ Your problem-solving abilities will increase as you gain more clarity about your life and relationships.

How will your relationships improve?

❖ This is yet another way to regroup and energise yourself. Your interactions with others will reflect your new perspective and outlook on life.

Reflection Time

Think

❖ Imagine or recall a situation where you felt frustrated with the people around you. Do you think that you would have felt less frustrated if you had taken five to ten minutes to spend on your own before going from one activity (work, school) to another?

Feel

❖ How does it feel to think that you can give yourself that time before going into a new situation? How does it feel to know that you can go into the new situation and enjoy it without feeling the frustration or negativity from the previous?

Act

❖ Allow yourself that time for self-care. Honour your need to be on your own. If it means being five to ten minutes late to a social situation, then so be it. You will thank yourself for it later, and you will enjoy the event more than you would have without those five to ten minutes to yourself.

Self care moment for today

Quiet and solitude n solitude

The mind gains strength and learns to lean upon itself. —Laurence Sterne

think

Could you enjoy social activities more if you spend a little time on your own beforehand?

feel

How does it feel to think that you can give yourself that time before going into a new situation?

act

Honour your need to be on your own

Add your own here:

think:

feel:

act:

CHAPTER SEVENTEEN

Being Alone Means Doing Activities You Can Do for Yourself and Nobody Else

The best part about being alone is that you really don't have to answer to anybody. You do what you want.

—Justin Timberlake

Justin's quote sums it up for me. When I spend time on my own, I don't have to answer to anybody but myself. Having said that, sometimes my internalised parents, teachers, and even my own thoughts get in my way and start whispering, "Why are you doing x-y-z when you could be working or doing a-b-c?"

It is then that I need to stick to my boundaries and what I've decided is the best for me at this point. I must silence these internal voices and thoughts and accept that right now, it's "me time," and all those other things can wait.

Spending time with others is essential. Although we are not islands, we are individuals in need of space to regroup, to re-energise, and know ourselves better. It's necessary to set clear boundaries and know what we need and want from ourselves, life, and our relationships.

When we don't know ourselves well, we end up compromising and meeting the needs and wants of others before we meet our own. Now, don't get me wrong. I'm not saying forget about everyone else or never do anything for anyone but yourself. It all needs to be balanced and consistent with what is right for you as an individual. Each of the following needs to be balanced:

❖ Being with people and being on your own

❖ Meeting your needs and the needs of others

❖ Knowing yourself well enough to listen to your instincts on whether to spend time with someone or reschedule

Knowing yourself means developing an awareness of how you think and feel. It requires you to build your emotional intelligence, which will help you decide what to do in your situations and relationships.

How will your life improve?

❖ Your self-esteem will increase because you will see that you are good company to yourself and that you are good enough (or better) as you are.

❖ You will be more self-reflective, more self-aware, and, therefore, more in tune with what you want and need. In turn, your boundaries will become even more apparent and more substantial.

❖ You will be less distracted if you are trying to solve a problem or come up with ideas for a particular situation. Sometimes we have too many voices speaking to us about the decisions we need to make—some things we need to figure out on our own.

How will your relationships improve?

❖ You come to understand why each relationship is important to you.

❖ You become grateful for the people who are in your life.

❖ You have the opportunity to reflect on those people who aren't in your life anymore and what you learned from those relationships.

❖ Your outlook on your relationships will be more positive and more in-depth. This will depend on the other person as well and where they are in their personal process.

Reflection Time

Think

❖ What does the prospect of spending time on your own bring up for you? What's the difference between being alone and being lonely?

Feel

❖ Take two minutes to find something in the room to focus on. It could be a plant, a book, or your shoes.

❖ Allow yourself to observe what happens to your body and mind when you focus on something for these two minutes. Do you feel more relaxed? Did your thoughts go quiet when you were focusing on the object?

Act

❖ If you are not accustomed to spending time on your own, set aside only ten minutes every day this week. Try doing some meditation, go out for a walk, lie down and close your eyes for that time, or catch up on a podcast. It could be any activity that you choose, but the goal is to do it without someone else there.

❖ As you get used to time on your own, add ten more minutes to your daily time until you find the right amount of time for you.

Self care moment for today

Being alone means doing activities that you can do for yourself and nobody else

The best part about being alone is that you really don't have to answer to anybody. — Justin Timberlake

think

What's the difference between being alone and being lonely?

feel

What happens to your body when you focus on an object for a few minutes

act

As you get used to time on your own, add ten more minutes to your daily time on your own.

Add your own here:

think:

feel:

act:

CHAPTER EIGHTEEN

—

Sleep Helps Us Process Information, Emotions, and Enhances Our Mental Health

It is a common experience that a problem difficult at night is resolved in the morning after the committee of sleep has worked on it.

—John Steinbeck

*The best bridge between despair and
hope is a good night's sleep.*

—E. Joseph Cossman

Why is sleep so great? Well, for many reasons. Firstly, the brain needs it to refresh, restart, and rest. That's the biological reason for sleep. The emotional and psychological basis for sleeping is that it helps to process intense emotions and think through difficult decisions to come up with solutions.

It could also be an escape of sorts. It's a way to restore anything that might be unbalanced or rocking the boat. I use sleep, yes, but I also talk to those closest to me and my therapist. It's the combination of these and other things that help keep my mental health in a good state.

Excessive sleep and failure to get out of bed might be a sign of something more serious like depression. This needs to be checked out by a professional or at least addressed in a way that helps you work through whatever is making you opt-out of daily life.

Getting adequate sleep equates to being able to function well in daily life. It allows you to have the mental space and energy to think about what's going on around you in a calmer, more rational way than you would if you were tired.

Being tired might lead you to overthink things or develop negative ways of coping that might not help resolve situations or deal with emotions proactively and helpfully.

Have you ever been so tired that you want to cry? A lack of rest can cause you to be irrational or agitated and affect your judgement and perception in negative ways.

How will your life improve?

❖ When you are well-rested, you have a better handle on whatever life throws at you.

❖ You will be in a positive mood and have a healthy level of energy.

❖ Your thought life will be more positive. You will be better able to combat harmful thoughts better than if you weren't getting enough sleep.

How will your relationships improve?

❖ When you are well-rested and have taken the time to re-energise, you will be in a better position to have a great time with others in social situations.

Reflection Time

Think

❖ Think about a time where you were sleep-deprived. What were you feeling, thinking, and doing? Were you more positive or negative about everyday situations? About yourself? About your relationships?

Feel

❖ Follow the routine as described in the *"Act"* section of this chapter.

❖ Observe how this all feels. Note how it affects your ability to sleep. Allow yourself to fall asleep and observe how you feel in the morning after a good night's sleep.

Act

❖ Plan a routine around going to bed earlier. Have a chamomile tea to help you relax. Leave your phone and other electronics outside your bedroom. Turn off all electronics and television at least one hour before going to bed. Do deep breathing when you are lying down. It will help your body to relax and allows you to fall asleep more easily. Tune your thoughts out by focusing on your breathing. It might take a few tries to fall asleep but keep at it.

Self care moment for today

Sleep helps us process information, emotions and enhances our mental health

The best bridge between despair and hope is a good night's sleep. ~ E. Joseph Cossman

think

How do you function when you are sleep-deprived? How is life affected?

feel

How would it feel to get at least 8 hours sleep every night.

act

Plan a routine around going to bed earlier.

Add your own here:

think:

feel:

act:

CHAPTER NINETEEN

Teach Others to Respect and Value You through Your Example

When you are content to be simply yourself and don't compare or compete, everyone will respect you.

—*Lao Tzu, Tao Te Ching*

I hope you have gathered respect and value for yourself as you've read and engaged in the practices in this book. Respect for yourself and others is very important. In this chapter, I'd like to talk a little bit more about this as a way of reinforcing what has already been said as well as to give you more food for thought.

Some people may have had parents who showed them how to respect and value themselves through their behaviour, but also by showing them they are respected and valued. Others may not have been as fortunate, but this doesn't mean you can't start now.

Respecting and valuing yourself means that you know how significant and valuable you are. Valuing yourself means that you understand your freedom to set boundaries that keep you safe, healthy, and happy. Having self-respect means knowing you are allowed to ask for what you need, as long as it doesn't negatively affect yourself or those around you.

Respecting and valuing yourself leads you to respect and appreciate those around you, therefore, positively impacting your relationships.

How will your life improve?

❖ Your level of self-love will increase.

❖ Setting boundaries will come naturally as you will do it out of organic respect and through valuing of yourself, your time, your space.

How will your relationships improve?

❖ You will choose the right relationships and let go of the wrong ones.

❖ You will be more open to others, as you will have the tools and skills in place to communicate your needs and boundaries better than ever.

Reflection Time

Think

❖ What was your upbringing like? Did you get the self-confidence, self-esteem, and self-respect you needed, either by those who set the example or adults in your life telling you that you were valued and respected?

❖ What was missing in this regard? What would you have liked to have happened instead?

Feel

❖ Reflecting on the questions above, how did it feel to be respected by others? How did it feel for you if you had the opposite experience?

Act

❖ Consider how you felt when you were growing up and compare it to how would you like to feel now? You have the power to change things for yourself—whether you want to gain more respect from yourself or others, or you need to start from scratch.

❖ Review the printables for each chapter in this book. Take note of how putting these into practice will help you develop that self-respect and value in yourself you need. Watch as it seeps into your relationships.

20 Self-Care Habits

Self care moment for today

Teach others to respect and value you through your example

"When you are content to be simply yourself and don't compare or compete, everyone will respect you." — Tao Tzu, Tao Te Ching

think

How has your upbringing affected who you are now?

feel

How did it feel to be respected or disrespected by others?

act

You have the power to change things for yourself. Use the tools in this book to get what you need.

Add your own here:

think:

feel:

act:

CHAPTER TWENTY

Get Rid of Toxic People: Keep Those Who Make You Happy

Toxic people attach themselves like cinder blocks tied to your ankles, and then invite you for a swim in their poisoned waters.

—John Mark Green

People inspire you, or they drain you. Pick them wisely.

—Hans F. Hasen

Stop letting people who do so little for you control
so much of your mind, feelings, and emotions.

—Will Smith

Letting go of toxic people in your life
is a big step in loving yourself.

—Hussein Nishah

For this final chapter, I couldn't just choose one quote to think about, that's why I've left four for you to ponder on above.

Throughout my life, I've "collected" toxic people. In my younger years, I might have put up with the toxicity due to needing acceptance and being afraid of being on my own or rejected by people.

As time went on, I learned to respect myself, my time, my feelings, and my thoughts. This helped me sort out the people who are good for me and those who are exhausting and make me feel awful.

Once I have identified those who are toxic in my life, I send them swiftly on their way. I have a small number of people I won't ever talk to or engage with again because they drain my energy and don't add any value to my life. This might seem harsh, but I'd rather do it this way than struggle with physical or mental health issues resulting from my interactions with and exposure to these people. They don't even realise or care what they do to us, but once we recognise it, we can do something about it and keep our lives safe and happy.

Toxic people come in all forms, shapes, and sizes. In general, poisonous people drain us. They take our energy by demanding a lot of our attention and demanding we do a lot for them whilst giving hardly anything to us.

More specifically, toxic people are cynical, enjoy drama, drag us into their issues and negativity, exploit our best intentions and goodwill, blame us for their misgivings and problems, and project their feelings and thoughts onto us—like we are the ones feeling and thinking for them, or we are the ones causing their problems.

It might be difficult to get rid of these people as they might be close relatives or have been in our lives for a long time. Once you have distanced yourself or altogether ended a relationship, you will feel the difference in your energy levels and emotional state.

How will your life improve?

❖ You will have more time, space, and energy for yourself.

❖ Your mental health will be intact or at least untouched by others' negativity and drama.

❖ Your life will be free of unnecessary negativity and drama.

How will your relationships improve?

❖ Your relationships will be healthy and happy.

❖ Your close relationships will be with people that add value to your life and those who respect you and love you for who you are, not by what you do for them.

❖ Your friendship circle might be smaller, but there will be more quality and depth to the friendships you do keep.

Reflection Time

Think

❖ Did someone come to mind whilst reading this chapter? What would you like to do about this person and your relationship with them?

Feel

❖ Imagine you decide to remove someone from your life that drains your energy and doesn't add value to your life. Imagine waking up without them in your life. How does that feel?

Act

❖ Review your friendships and relationships and work out who adds value to your life and who doesn't. Take note of those who don't add much but take a lot. Decide whether you will get rid of the relationship, distance yourself, or give them a final chance whilst setting more precise boundaries with them. Sometimes there are options, other times, we need to cut them off.

Self care moment for today

Get rid of toxic people

think

Is there a relationship that is not healthy for you in your life?

feel

How would it feel to stop feeling drained by that person?

act

Review your relationships and work out who adds value to your life, and who doesn't.

Add your own here:

think:

feel:

act:

A Final Word

Through practicing all of the above, your life and relationships will improve

I am so glad you have come to the final chapter of this book. It means that you are on your way to improving your self-care activities, which, in turn, will strengthen your relationship with yourself and those around you.

We have talked about setting boundaries, making time to be in nature, as well as what to do with relationships that might not be ideal or right for us.

Mainly, I wish these ideas would improve your life. I hope the printables (you will be able to download them from my website if you have the printed copy) will be a friendly reminder on your wall, fridge, or wherever you put them. I hope the ideas I've given you in this book are helpful and you put them into practice.

I would love to hear from you if you need any extra support for your self-care or any other issues you might be going through. I also have a blog you might find helpful. I write about a variety of topics, and I welcome feedback, comments, and suggestions for future posts.

Do come over to the Facebook group I've created especially for my readers. In time, I hope it becomes a supportive community. It's what I consider a "corner" of the web that provides space to reflect, share experiences, and learn from one another.

Wishing you the best in your self-care journey and hoping to be a part of it in one way or another!

—Karin

About the Author

Karin Brauner is passionate about helping people get on track—or back on track—in their personal and professional lives through practical tools and inspirational conversations in a variety of settings.

Karin teaches tools that she's learned and developed throughout her own life. She knows how hard things can get, but also how great things can be once you move through to the other side.

She now shares the knowledge she's gained through various mediums to show people a path to better self-care and support when processing their past and working out their present so they can lead an improved life and thrive in their personal and professional relationships.

Connect at karinbrauneronline.co.uk

Acknowledgements

I would like to thank . . .

- ❖ God for giving me this life to live this life and the opportunity to do what I love to do.

- ❖ My husband, Shaun, for being patient with me and supporting me in all the things I get up to— like writing this book.

- ❖ The people who purchase and benefit from this book. You are the reason I wrote it.

- ❖ My lovely book reviewers, who kindly agreed to review my book even before the final copy was ready to print.

- ❖ The people who were—and those who still are—in my life, who taught me everything I've written in this book—those who have had a positive impact, but also those who have had a less positive one and led me to develop those strengths within me that I wouldn't have discovered otherwise.

❖ Those situations in life that led me to improve my life and relationships and eventually write this book.

❖ My clients and those I've been lucky, blessed, and humbled to help in their self-care and life journeys.

Resources

Keep on top of your self-care habits

Download your printables for each chapter of the book

karinbrauneronline.co.uk/printables

Let's continue the conversation

Join the facebook group today!

facebook.com/groups/20habits

Self-Care Coaching

Delve deeper into your self-care journey...
The book has changed lives.
The Programmes will take you even further

Disclaimer: There is no quick fix!
A mindset change will take a bit of
time but it's not impossible.

This mindset re-set will
change your whole life. Trust
me, I've seen it in my own
life, and in the lives of my
clients!

Why should we fit in a box
someone else made
somewhere in the ether?

Truth is – we don't!

By working on our boundaries and learning how to meet our
needs, we get to know who we really are and how we want to
live our lives to the fullest.

https://karinbrauneronline.co.uk/self-care/

Mini-Courses

Did the topics touched upon in the novel leave you wanting to find out more about how to deal with them and other topics?

I've created mini-courses with lots of information, reflection points, print-outs, check-lists, and more.

Creating and Living a more Compassionate Life

Anger: Fear it or befriend it

Find Your Own Way To Grieve

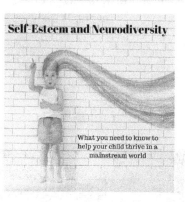

Self-Esteem and Neurodiversity

What you need to know to help your child thrive in a mainstream world

karinbrauneronline.co.uk/mini-courses

Mini-Courses

Did the topics touched upon in the novel leave you wanting to find out more about how to deal with them and other topics?

I've created mini-courses with lots of information, reflection points, print-outs, check-lists, and more.

Creating and Living a more Compassionate Life

Anger: Fear it or befriend it

Find Your Own Way To Grieve

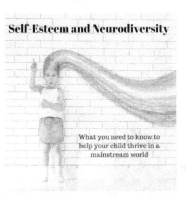

Self-Esteem and Neurodiversity

What you need to know to help your child thrive in a mainstream world

karinbrauneronline.co.uk/mini-courses